THE BLOOD-STAINED TRAIL

The Voice of the Martyrs

with Riley K. Smith

VOM
BOOKS

China: The Blood-Stained Trail

VOM Books
P.O. Box 443
Bartlesville, OK 74005-0443

Previously published by Living Sacrifice Books, an imprint of The Voice of the Martyrs.

ISBN 978-0-88264-029-7

Edited by Lynn Copeland

Cover by Lookout Design

Page design and layout by Genesis Group

Printed in the United States of America

Reprinted April 2013

Unless otherwise indicated, Scripture references are from the *New King James* version, © 1979, 1980, 1982 by Thomas Nelson Inc., Publishers, Nashville, Tennessee.

"The government does not wish to create martyrs. They make religion uncontrollable."

—A COMMUNIST GOVERNMENT OFFICIAL IN BEIJING

"*But I want you to know, brethren, that the things which happened to me have actually turned out for the furtherance of the gospel, so that it has become evident to the whole palace guard, and to all the rest, that my chains are in Christ; and most of the brethren in the Lord, having become confident by my chains, are much more bold to speak the word without fear... For I know that this will turn out for my deliverance through your prayer and the supply of the Spirit of Jesus Christ, according to my earnest expectation and hope that in nothing I shall be ashamed, but with all boldness, as always, so now also Christ will be magnified in my body, whether by life or by death.*"

—THE APOSTLE PAUL, martyred in 69 A.D.
(Philippians 1:12–14,19,20)

CONTENTS

ACKNOWLEDGMENTS

I would like to thank several individuals who were directly or indirectly involved in the development of this book. First of all, thank you, Bob Service, for the materials on the Three-Self Church, Catholic Patriotic Association, SARA, and PSB. Well done!

I thank my daughters who played heartily and rested half-heartedly while I researched, outlined, and hammered out the first draft. May you be so in love with Jesus that you will go wherever He calls! I also thank my husband who patiently listened to my challenges and discoveries in the process of writing this book. Thank you, Mom, for your review of the first draft and encouragement to persevere through the mounds of research and painstaking task of revision.

Thanks to Todd Nettleton at The Voice of the Martyrs for the very helpful and thoughtful feedback on the second draft. Thank you, Bob Fu, for answering my questions on the final draft. It was a privilege to attend your ceremony in Washington, D.C., where you received the John Leland Religious Liberty Award from Dr. Richard Land of the Ethics & Religious Liberty Commission of the Southern Baptist Convention. May God continue to bless the church in China through your words and work with China Aid Association!

Thank you, Pastor Mark Carey of Fellowship Bible Church, Winchester, Virginia, for the additional resources on Kublai Khan. And thank you, Lynn Copeland, for your excellent questions and comments to further refine the message of this book.

Finally, I am thankful for the testimonies of China's martyrs. Their faithful witness led them into the arms of Christ, and they now wear the crown.

Lord Jesus, may these pages full of stories of courage and grace in the face of death launch Your people into deeper fellowship—and riskier ventures—with You.

As the apostle Paul wrote, "According to my earnest expectation and hope that in nothing I shall be ashamed, but with all boldness, as always, so now also Christ will be magnified in my body, whether by life or by death" (Philippians 1:20).

May Christ be exalted with this book!

RILEY K. SMITH

INTRODUCTION:
THE BLOOD-STAINED TRAIL

His heart burned to reach the lost in China. Thousands were dying every day without hearing the message of salvation, and he wanted to do something about it. But that came with a risk. Auguste Chapdelaine of France knew that many missionaries who pioneered into China with the gospel faced a dangerous end: Many were beaten, imprisoned, and even killed for bringing this message that challenged ancestor worship, Buddhism, and Confucianism. Still, he needed to go.

So in the mid nineteenth century, Auguste left behind a grieving family. He buried his sister, kissed his family good-bye, and boarded a ship bound for China.

His arrival on the outskirts of China was neither the end of his journey nor the challenges he would face. Only three days into his trek to Guangxi province, he was robbed of all his possessions, forcing him to turn back. His second attempt to reach Guangxi led him through the city of Guiyang, where a Chinese believer taught him the language.

Auguste finally arrived in Guangxi. He fell on his knees to thank God for bringing him there and offered his life to the work God had given him. He was there only ten days before the local government learned of his presence and arrested him. After spending about three weeks in prison, he was released and continued to share the gospel.

In two years Auguste led hundreds to Christ, but his mission in China was soon cut short.

In 1856, a Chinese woman whose husband had recently become a Christian got into a disagreement with her spouse and went to the magistrate, who hated Christians, and informed him of Auguste and his mission work. At the time, foreigners were confined to five treaty ports that were opened after the signing of the Treaty of Nanking. Auguste's presence outside an agreed-upon port angered the Chinese, and this woman's report was more than likely the evidence the magistrate needed to take action against the Christians.

Soldiers were ordered to apprehend Auguste. Chinese believers insisted he go into hiding. He protested, knowing the danger it would bring them. Finally, he gave in.

About two dozen Chinese Christians were arrested and put in chains. A number of women, relatives of those arrested, went to Auguste. "What do we do? Do we ask for their release?" they asked him, when a new believer stepped up and offered to accompany the women. They presented their case before the magistrate, who promptly had them all arrested.

Auguste was no longer safe. His hiding place was discovered. When the chief guard entered his room, Auguste was face down in prayer and was soon led away.

Auguste and the Chinese believers were beaten and interrogated. The new believer who had accompanied the women was threatened by the magistrate, who warned, "If you do not forsake God, and renounce your religion, your head shall be cut off."

The man courageously replied, "The mandarin [magistrate] may cut off my head, and not only mine, but that of my wife and my children. But to renounce my religion, the religion of the God of heaven, to cease to address my prayers to Him—ah, never! I will never be guilty of so black a treason. Mandarin, cut off my head, if you wish, but I will never apostatize."

The magistrate ordered him to be whipped. After seeing that the new believer would not change his mind, the magistrate had him decapitated.

A Chinese woman named Agnes, whom Auguste had asked to teach women and young girls about the Christian faith, was brought before the magistrate and given a similar threat of death. She replied, "Cause me to die if such be your will, but I will never renounce the religion of teacher

Ma [what the Chinese called Auguste], since his is the religion of the God of heaven!"

The woman was placed in a cage near Auguste and died days later from the torture she endured.

It was Auguste's turn. "Deny Christ!" the magistrate demanded of Auguste.

The Christian leader replied, "My religion is the true religion, and I cannot betray it." The magistrate ordered Auguste locked in a cangue (a piece of wood that serves as a yoke confining the head and arms), but not until he was whipped one hundred times on the cheeks with a strip of leather, knocking out his teeth and breaking his jaw. His torturers didn't stop and caned him three hundred times.

Auguste silently endured the affliction. "It must be the magic!" his torturers insisted, and ordered a dog be sacrificed and its blood poured over Auguste to break the spell.

With Auguste near death, the soldiers dragged him back to his cell. On the way, Auguste began to hold himself upright and walk on his own. Since he was previously unable to move after being so brutally beaten, his renewed strength shocked the guards. When they asked him how this was possible, Auguste gave the glory to God. Convinced that it was magic, the magistrate again ordered Auguste into the cangue where he died during the night of February 29, 1856.

Many believe that the men who martyred Auguste tore out his heart and examined it, hoping to find his courage. They found nothing but flesh, so they tore it to pieces, cooked it, and ate it.

Auguste Chapdelaine and many other faithful missionaries to China are a part of this blood-stained trail. Were their lives a waste? Was their passion for China nothing but a zealous whim to prove something to themselves or others? Was their intent to spread their Western ideas in order to expand the trade interests of Britain, America, France, or other European nations? Or were their hearts genuinely seeking to add more names to Jesus' Book of Life? One can try to argue their reasons for going, but one cannot overlook the harvest of souls that multiplied throughout China's history in the wake of persecution.

Throughout history, many Chinese Christians like Blind Chang, Watchmen Nee, Jiang Zongxiu, and many thousands more have also followed this blood-stained trail. Today, they continue to risk all to take the gospel to their fellow countrymen and even to those outside China's borders. Though today the government doesn't confine Christians to treaty ports, their gospel message is confined to the four walls of government-approved churches. Those who dare to take the gospel outside the church are often arrested, beaten, and imprisoned. Many are sentenced to *lao gai*, "reeducation through labor," and some have been sentenced to life in prison. But their overcoming courage in the face of persecution sets them apart from the tainted view of martyrs the world gives us today: one that takes away the lives of others. Christ's martyrs give courage and life.

This book is a brief overview of China's blood-stained trail, offering a glimpse of the afflictions and overcoming courage of Christ's Body from its first recorded arrival to the present day. We invite you to join your brothers and sisters in Christ on this journey that will take you through significant events in China's history that directly affected the church. In these events, you will meet men and women, as well as youth, who refused to deny Christ when confronted with torture, prison, and even death. But before you read further, you must know what this book is not: It is not an attempt to oversimplify China's multilayered culture, history, and politics by giving one-dimensional answers to complex questions. It is a look into the hearts of those who dared to go and who dared to tell throughout its rich and complex history.

May the testimonies in this book fill your heart with courage to stand firm for Christ and view your life's setbacks as an opportunity for God to be glorified in and through you!

CHINA TODAY

Disturbing the Social Order

The village market was full of people. As Jiang Zongxiu and her mother-in-law, Mrs. Tan, made their way through the crowds handing out gospel tracts, they knew that each person holding that piece of paper was a potential new member of God's family. The excitement ran through them, until Public Security Bureau (PSB) officials approached them and ordered them to the county detention center. These women troubled officials. Their message of a Higher Power that rules over the government was a threat to its existence, and they had to be stopped.

Jiang and Mrs. Tan were accused of "suspected spreading of rumor and disturbing the social order," by "distributing Christian literature to the masses in the market." They were sentenced to fifteen days detention.

On the night they were arrested, June 17, 2004, Jiang and Mrs. Tan were interrogated by police until the following morning. During a break in their interrogation, Jiang was able to speak with Mrs. Tan and told her the grueling details: Police had kicked her, torn off her shoes, and pulled out her hair. At one time, Mrs. Tan even saw a policeman kick her. Mrs. Tan would never again see her daughter-in-law alive.

When Mrs. Tan was released from the detention center that afternoon, she was told Jiang had died. The official report on her death made it clear that her death did not result from "outside forces" or poisons. Her reported cause of death? "Heart failure."

Mrs. Tan and Zhang Zhenghua, Jiang's husband, were puzzled by Jiang's sudden death. "We were married ten years ago. I have been working in Chongqing to sustain the family," explained Zhang. "All the work of my family—farming the land, feeding the livestock, raising our four-year-old, and taking care of my parents—had to be done

Jiang Zongxiu

by her alone. She had never been afflicted by any diseases."

"I want my mommy," cried her young son over and over.

The PSB wasted no time covering up the truth of Jiang's death, notifying Jiang's family that her body would be cremated. Still suspicious, Zhang demanded an autopsy.

During the autopsy, Jiang's sister-in-law secretly took photographs. Her body bore scars on her legs and neck. As further proof, a policeman at the funeral home said, "She doesn't need an autopsy, because it is very obvious that she was beaten to death."

Jiang and Mrs. Tan's trip to the market to share God's Word cost Jiang her life. How many more Chinese believers will be imprisoned or martyred for bringing further "disturbances" to China's atheistic agenda?

CHRISTIANITY'S ARRIVAL:
THE TRAIL BEGINS

Given China's history of suspicion toward foreigners, it's remarkable that China's first missionaries had great favor with the emperor. Perhaps their new ideas and lifestyle of worshiping a Higher Power intrigued him.

A stone in the modern-day city of Xian tells the story of a sect of Christianity officially setting foot in China. Standing almost 10 feet high and over 3 feet wide, the monument recounts the arrival of a Nestorian named Alopen in China's capital in 635 A.D.

The Nestorians were a faction of the church that believed Christ existed as two distinct persons: as the man and as the divine. A man named Nestorius began this sect around the fifth century and was condemned at the Council of Ephesus in 431 A.D. The Nestorians were considered heretics based on their beliefs that eerily resemble Arianism—a heresy that plagued the church in the fourth century A.D., which led to the Council of Nicea in 325 A.D. Nestorians do not believe that Christ the Divine suffered on the cross; Christ the man did. If the Nestorians refused to accept that Christ the Divine suffered on the cross, is it possible this false belief caused them to refuse to endure suffering when China's emperors incited persecution against them? Read on, and you decide.

Alopen arrived during the Tang dynasty's "golden age," when China made many cultural strides in such areas as art, literature, trade, and technology. Emperor Taizung welcomed him. Taizung issued an edict of "universal toleration" three years later, granting the Nestorians permission to spread Christianity throughout China. The first Christian church was built in the capital, Chang'an. Emperor Taizung used funds from his treasury for the construction of the church while also funding the building of Buddhist and Taoist temples.

However, the Nestorians' favor among China's emperors soon faltered.

Nestorian tablet

In 649, Emperor Taizung died, and his son Gaozu succeeded him on the throne. Although he continued to give the Nestorians great favor, he made the mistake of taking one of his father's concubines—Wu Hou—into his household. Blood-thirsty and ambitious, Wu aptly earned her nickname of the "wicked witch" of traditional Chinese history when she bore the emperor a son and murdered the newborn only to accuse the empress whose reputation was now tainted with the scandal of the murder. Wu took her place but wasn't finished with the ruined empress: She had her hands and feet cut off and left her to die.

Empress Wu overshadowed her husband's throne for almost three decades until his death in 683. She deposed her sons from the throne and set up a new dynasty in her name. She took a Buddhist monk as a lover and declared Buddhism the state religion in 691, after which it seems she began privately promoting hostility toward Christians. In 698, persecution became apparent when mobs destroyed a Christian church in the eastern capital of Loyang—a Buddhist stronghold for 600 years. Persecution finally hit the western capital of Chang'an, where angry mobs were permitted to attack the Nestorians' first church.

After the "wicked witch" Wu died, her grandson took the throne. During his reign, the Nestorian Monument records that church buildings were restored. In 744, missionaries began to arrive from Persia. The church once more had favor with the emperor.

During the next two hundred years, the number of Nestorians flourished and faded.

Thus marks the beginning of China's blood-stained trail. The Nestorians and their subsequent decline would cycle again during the next several centuries with the invasion of the Mongols and the arrival of the Polo brothers.

CATHOLIC MISSIONARIES:
THE TRAIL CONTINUES

China was no longer safe. Its borders had been breached by the Mongols, who became the first foreign dynasty to govern China. But these barbarians from the north that ruled China from 1279 until 1368 weren't the source of the church's troubles. Western traders arrived and along with them Catholic missionaries threatened the Nestorians' centuries-long monopoly on missions. And with this tension over "religious territory" came conflict that plagued the church from within followed by persecution from without. Such were the milestones—and roadblocks—as these foreign messengers journeyed along the trail.

History tells us very little about China's Christians when the Mongols occupied China. One of the most important accounts is Marco Polo's journey to Mongol China. However, it was his father and uncle who preceded him to China.

The Polo brothers (Marco's father and uncle) first arrived in China around 1265, and were welcomed by Kublai Khan. Kublai expressed so much interest in Christianity that he had the Polo brothers carry a letter to the pope, requesting a hundred educated men to teach the people about Christianity and Western science. Kublai Khan said, "So shall I be baptized, and when I am baptized, all my barons and lords will be baptized, and their subjects will receive baptism and so there will be more Christians here than in your own countries." At the same time, he invited Lamas from Tibet to share the message of Buddhism as well. Tibet responded by sending monks; however, the arrival of Christian missionaries took a sobering turn.

It took the Polo brothers three years to return to their homeland in Europe where they remained two years before they returned to China. However, the pope did not respond with a hundred missionaries but with two Dominicans. During their journey, the Dominican duo became so troubled at the outbreak of war that they returned home. Therefore, the Polo brothers, this time with Marco, finished their journey to Mongol China without any gospel messengers. Unfortunately Kublai Khan, who seemed to be seeking the truth, had died before the first Catholic missionaries arrived in the late thirteenth century. Although some wonder if Kublai's request for missionaries was rooted in an interest to build political alliances and expand the Mongols' understanding of the world, it was a missed opportunity for one of the most powerful men in Asia to learn about Jesus Christ.

Marco Polo's time in China uncovered widespread Nestorian communities scattered across the empire. The Nestorians had reentered Chinese public and political life with the Mongols, quickly rising in favor and status with the government. However, their influence within the

government and over the church would be challenged with the arrival of the first Catholic missionary.

Catholic Missionaries Arrive

After the death of Kublai Khan in 1294, Catholic
missionaries, including John of Montecorvino,
arrived in Peking (Beijing). The Nestorians viewed
the new missionaries with great contempt. To
them, the Catholics were competitors and "schis-
matics." When the highest ranking Nestorian
Christian converted to Roman Catholicism, the
Nestorians were furious, accusing John of Montecorvino of being nothing but "a spy, magician, and
deceiver of men." The Nestorians could do nothing about it: Catholic missionaries kept arriving.

Despite the opposition, John of Montecorvino persevered. In 1299, he built a cathedral in
Beijing. By 1305, he had won as many as 6,000
converts. By the time he died, the Mongol dynasty was crumbling. The last Mongol emperor
was considered lazy and unwise, his prime minister was openly anti-Chinese, and the Nestorians
who rose within the Mongol government began
to turn from their beliefs. Many embraced Confucianism, a few Taoism.

The Chinese finally rebelled and kicked out
the barbaric Mongols. The new China was to be
purely China-centered, following in the teachings
of Confucius, and independent of foreign influence and control. This dynasty became known as

the Ming. Since the Nestorians and Catholics were considered foreigners as were the Mongols, it is believed they were massacred along with their Mongol sympathizers. When the Jesuits arrived two hundred years later, they saw no sign of Christianity on the blood-stained trail.

The Jesuits Begin Their Journey

China's new policies of isolationism and nationalism made it very difficult, if not impossible, for missionaries to enter China. Around 1557, Jesuits arrived and set up a base at Macao, a peninsula in South China. More than twenty-five years would pass before they succeeded in establishing a base in China's mainland in a small village east of Guangzhou (formerly called Canton). Matteo Ricci, Alessandro Valignano, and Michele Ruggieri were three Italians who spearheaded a missionary advance into China, which some say has forever changed the balance of religion in East Asia.

The Jesuits had a driving desire to gain further inroads into China's interior. It did not happen until 1583, a year after Ricci joined the men, when a viceroy invited them to live in the county seat of Shaoqing near Guangzhou and offered to build them a chapel.

Unconventional and ahead of his time in his approach to missions, Ricci immersed himself in the culture and believed the future of the Chinese church was in the training of indigenous believers. This raised eyebrows within the Jesuit order. Feeling it was necessary to attract Chinese attention by demonstrating expertise in areas that interested them, Ricci taught mathematics and astronomy and created a map of the world that drew the Chinese out of their ethnocentric view. But Ricci longed to go to Beijing and see the emperor. He believed he could convince the emperor to open China to the gospel.

In 1589, a viceroy drove him out of the village. However, this only moved him closer to the capital and furthered the gospel, as Ricci built another church. This time he used Chinese architecture because it was less expensive and stressed his belief that Christianity was not confined to Western culture.

China today

Six years later, Ricci neared Beijing when he relocated to the province of Jiangxi and was later allowed to move the Jesuit mission farther north to Nanjing. Ricci reported a hundred converts a year within two years of his arrival. His time there was very valuable for the Chinese church when Ricci met and discipled a Chinese convert named Paul Hsu, whose ministry was effective. He, along with Michael Yang and Leon Li, became known as "the three pillars of the early Chinese church."

Ricci died without fulfilling his dream of meeting the emperor and convincing him to open up China to the gospel. However, he did breach the borders forbidden to missionaries, lead many to Christ, and use unconventional methods to share the gospel. Such methods and convictions would later cause conflict in the church.

Adam Schall succeeded Ricci and fulfilled Ricci's dream of meeting the emperor. After Muslim mathematicians miscalculated an eclipse, Adam Schall, Paul Hsu, and Leon Li—known as reputable astronomers and mathematicians—were given the task of reforming the Bureau of Mathematics. Such a miscalculation was considered unforgivable, given China's reliance on the stars for guidance in all matters of life. However, their rise in status in the imperial court brought with it scorn and jealousy, leading to persecution.

In 1616, an official in Nanjing started an anti-Christian campaign. Jesuit missionaries were thrown in prison. The following year the emperor was coerced into signing an anti-Christian edict. Many Chinese sympathized with the Christians and hid them in their homes. Remarkably, just two of the missionaries in Nanjing were cruelly treated: One was flogged, and both were caged and paraded almost a thousand miles to Guangzhou, where they were released.

Throughout this time, the Ming dynasty had been falling apart, and finally collapsed when the Manchurians from the northeast broke through the Great Wall, conquering Beijing in 1644. However, this was the first time the church didn't go down with the crumbling dynasty, as happened when the Tang and Mongol dynasties fell.

Schall found favor with the new Manchurian emperor who gave him and the Jesuits a piece of land, a church, and a place to live in the capital. This was the first public church building since John of Montecorvino and the Mongol dynasty.

Schall's imperial favor faded three years after the emperor died. Several charges were made against Schall, who was arrested just one day after suffering a stroke and was then sentenced to death. However, the appearance of a comet and several natural disasters forced Chinese officials, in a culture traditionally prone to superstition, to reconsider Schall's arrest and release him. He died soon after.

Roadblocks: The Controversy Over Rites and Religious Territory

After Schall's death, a church controversy, rooted decades earlier, came to a head. Called the "Rites Controversy," debate arose over how much Christianity should adapt itself to words and cultures influenced by other religions. Many Jesuits wrestled with Ricci's views on accommodating cultures for the purpose of making inroads to share the gospel. Others argued over how to translate "God" into Chinese. This rift over rites would later come back to haunt the Jesuits.

Much like the Nestorians' bout with "territorialism" when the Catholics arrived, the advent of the Spanish Franciscans and Dominicans had a similar effect on the Jesuits. The newly arrived missionaries also felt the Jesuits' accommodation to Chinese culture as questionable, if not weak. Despite the conflict, the church was growing.

Schall's successor, Ferdinand Verbiest, ascended in favor with the imperial court, leading to some easing of restrictions that hadn't been experienced in decades. It was the 1671 edict that granted the church the right to own land. Preaching was allowed as long as it didn't contradict the country's well-being, and Chinese were still forbidden to convert to Christianity. However, in 1692, Emperor Kangxi finally issued an order tolerating Christianity.

In 1705, the Jesuits convinced the emperor to make China a Catholic state. When they presented the idea to the pope, he rejected it, stating "the emperor could not be a Christian and continue to worship his ancestors."

The "Rites Controversy" continued to simmer until it came to a boiling conclusion when the Jesuits involved the emperor. This infuriated Rome. (It wouldn't be until 1742 that this conflict would finally come to an end with the pope issuing a Papal Bull.)

For the next hundred years, persecutions continued sporadically. With the Jesuits falling from "imperial grace," Christianity was in the process of being left without a somewhat sympathetic ear in the government.

Emperor Kangxi's successor, Yung-cheng, ascended the throne in 1724, and issued an edict against Christianity by expelling missionaries and ordering them to Guangzhou. He declared Christianity a false religion and considered God becoming a man foolish. But the "driving out" of missionaries did not end with the edict. During the persecution of 1746 to 1748, he ordered that foreign priests be hunted down. Missionaries either went into hiding or left. Churches were destroyed, and many Chinese converts recanted their faith. However, many missionaries later sneaked back into China to baptize new believers and visit those they had led to Christ. Adding insult to injury, Pope Clement XIV dissolved the Jesuit order, creating questions and confusion among the church.

The onset of the nineteenth century did not improve matters for the Chinese church. Church leaders were still hunted down and executed. Some dared to stay, like Andrew Li, who traveled to Sichuan province, where he survived prison. For six years he was the only priest in the province.

At the end of the Opium Wars (1839–1842 and 1856–1860), China was forced to sign treaties keeping foreign missionaries outside the scope of the Chinese government's authority. The treaties may have brought peace or momentary physical safety to foreign missionaries, but they created resentment among the Chinese who associated the missionaries with both the opium trade and the humiliating war.

This resentment would build and later be unleashed on the church in China, but not before Protestant missionaries arrived, driving the gospel into the heart of China.

STORY OF PERSECUTION FROM HISTORY

The Faithful Franciscans

The seven Franciscans went to what was known as the outskirts of civilization. The treacherous mountain terrain and bone-dry deserts couldn't deter what these fourteenth-century Franciscans had to share with the citizens of Ili (modern-day Xinjiang). Led by Richard of Burgundy, France, these mission-minded men from around the known world lived like nomads as they witnessed many embracing the message of salvation.

Not long after they reached Ili, the prince of Ili became ill. One of the Franciscans, Francis of Alexandria, had experience as a surgeon and was able to treat him. The prince recovered and was so grateful that he, as well as his father (the khan), allowed the missionaries not only to preach freely, but also to instruct the Mongol prince's eight-year-old son in Christianity.

Several years later, the Franciscans' favor came to a sudden stop when the khan was poisoned by one of the princes in his family, a Muslim fanatic who took the throne and ordered all Christians to convert to Islam. Those who refused would face death. Knowing the risk, the believers courageously "professed their faith" and continued to gather for worship.

The seven missionaries were arrested, chained together, and forced to stand before a mob of raging Muslims who whipped them and then cut off their noses and ears. Still, the seven men were unstoppable, praising God and preaching the gospel to anyone who dared look upon their formless, bloodied faces.

Angered at their refusal to deny Christ, the mob cut off their heads and then proceeded to attack the Franciscans' convent.

They showed no mercy toward ethnic believers, who were thrown in prison and tortured. Many died, but those who survived were released when a Mongol chief overthrew and killed the self-proclaimed ruler.

The Ili church survived, and the gospel was still being preached there four hundred years later.

THE FIRST PROTESTANTS:
THE TRAIL EXPANDS

Robert Morrison prayed that God would send him to a mission field where "the difficulties were greatest and most insurmountable." Morrison's prayer was answered, and he became the first Protestant missionary to China, arriving in 1807. Since Britain's East India Company had a policy against carrying missionaries on their ships, Morrison, a citizen of Great Britain, went to America for help but was met with more skepticism. When the ship owner asked if he expected to make an impression on the idolatry of the great Chinese empire, Morrison replied, "No, sir, but I expect that God will."

At the time Morrison set foot in China, all mission activity was still illegal. The sentence for evangelizing was strangulation, so Morrison chose to keep a low profile and dressed like one of the Chinese, even wearing a false pigtail to blend in. He later gave up the disguise, thinking it only roused suspicion, and dressed like other Westerners who had come to China on business.

An 1812 edict made it illegal to teach a foreigner Chinese and carried with it a sentence of death, but his knowledge of the language led him to translate the Old and New Testaments into Chinese. Though preaching was often expected of missionaries, which at that time would get him deported, he felt providing a Bible for the Chinese would leave a greater, and lasting, impact. In

1819, the Bible was finally published in twenty-one volumes, but not without its share of challenges. Morrison had to manage the printing and cutting of the woodblocks (a printing method used in China that precedes the printing press), which were sometimes destroyed by white ants and hostile Chinese magistrates. He persevered to print the Word for the Chinese even when imperial edicts were issued against Christians and when persecution was stirred up against his small group of faithful followers of Christ.

Hoping China would one day open back up to missionaries, Morrison proposed setting up a missionary base outside the country to train workers. His request was granted, and William Milne was sent to lead it. Milne led a Chinese man named Liang Fa to Christ. Despite persecution, Liang would make a significant contribution to Protestant missions in his lifetime.

Liang was ordained by Morrison and was the first ordained Chinese Protestant evangelist. However, his work in evangelism was interrupted by government persecution, and he was exiled to Malacca for about four years. In 1839, he returned and baptized four new believers and led Sunday worship. He was imprisoned and beaten when the government discovered his work on gospel tracts. He was later released and continued to print and distribute tracts.

After Morrison died in 1834, many more Protestant missionaries followed in his footsteps. And with the increase in missionaries came an increase in Chinese converts. Britain's victory over China in the Opium War (also called the Anglo-Chinese War) forced China to sign peace treaties giving missionaries the freedom to work in China. However, Chinese resentment toward foreigners was building, causing Christianity to be viewed as a tool of Western expansion and ideas. Any Chinese who embraced Christianity was considered a traitor.

Protestant missions' first martyr was Walter Lowrie, who sailed to China in 1842 at the age of 22. He arrived at Macau, where he spent his time learning the language while studying the Scriptures. In 1845, he went to Ningbo. That same year, a printing press was imported, and gospel tracts and portions of Scripture clicked off the press and were distributed.

Lowrie was in Shanghai attending a mission conference when word reached him that he needed to return to Ningbo. During his voyage, pirates seized the ship and threw Lowrie overboard to eliminate witnesses. As they pushed him over the side, Lowrie tossed onto the deck a copy of the Bible in Hebrew, Greek, and English. He bobbed in the water briefly and then drowned. No one knows if one of the pirates picked up the book and turned to Christ.

Lowrie's premature death at the age of twenty-eight was not in vain. In 1850, his father published a book called *Memoirs of the Rev. Walter*

M. Lowrie, Missionary to China, inspiring many to commit their lives to Christ.

In a sermon he had given on March 14, 1847, in Ningbo, Lowrie admonished, "May God grant, beloved hearers, that you and I may persevere unto the end, and enter at last on the rest that remaineth for the people of God, and the inheritance that shall be given to his sons!" Lowrie persevered to the end and entered God's rest.

In 1866, a new wave of missionaries breached the borders of China. Hudson Taylor's China Inland Mission (CIM) arrived with a total of eighteen volunteers. Like the Jesuit missions pioneer, Matteo Ricci, Taylor's work was considered unconventional at the time. Not only was it not financially supported by a specific Protestant denomination, but his staff of volunteers was full of single women. They went to areas of China considered "unreached" with few or no Christians. And like Ricci and Morrison, his workers embraced Chinese dress and hairstyle, causing them to be mocked as "the pigtail mission."

Taylor's work made waves among churches in the West. He appealed to Protestant denominations to send workers, and many responded to his plea. The Chinese church was growing. However, the humiliation suffered by the Chinese as a result of the Opium War was also growing and would climax at the dawn of the twentieth century in a mass murder of Christians. But the blood shed in the name of Christ merely prepared the soil for more souls to receive the seed of the Word, which would lead to one of the fastest growing churches in the world today.

SECRET SOCIETIES

"Secret political Societies have existed in many countries: but in no other part of the world have they flourished and exerted so much influence for ill, as in China."

—WILLIAM STANTON, *The Triad Society, or Heaven and Earth Association*

They're elusive, politically motivated, and often-times criminally minded. Many felt invincible, unable to be harmed. Others claimed to have special powers, seeing more than the physical eye. These were China's Secret Societies, responsible for murdering countless missionaries and Chinese believers to further their cause.

Christians were also caught in the middle of government crackdowns on Secret Societies, like the one involving the White Lotus Society (called Pah Lian). With Buddhist roots, the White Lotus Society was politically motivated, aiming to destroy certain dynasties and reestablish others. By the early 1600s, the Society was causing unrest across China. When they finally threatened Beijing, the emperor took action to stop them, demanding its leaders be arrested to end the secret group. But this was a challenge, considering the difficulty of identifying members of the White Lotus Society.

In the meantime, Catholic influence grew with such missionaries as Matteo Ricci, who gained great favor with the empire through his expertise in mathematics and astronomy. Nevertheless, the number of Catholic converts concerned the government. A senior government official named Shen Que used the crackdown on the White Lotus Society to issue his own manifesto against Secret Societies throughout the empire. But his version called for the arrest and torture of "all who would not denounce their faith in the Lord of heaven"—Christians!

Local officials ransacked churches. Many Christians were chained and taken to prison where they were tortured and coerced into confessing to crimes they didn't commit. Some died from the persecution. Foreign missionaries were forced to leave China, although many secretly remained.

Almost three centuries later, a group of Protestant missionaries working in Guitan, Fujian province, and retreating at Huasang village was attacked by a different Secret Society known as the Vegetarians. The Vegetarians were an odd crew of insurgents. Anti-government rebels who claimed to abstain from meat, the Vegetarians would bring nuts, seeds, and fruit as part of their worship ritual.

The Vegetarians had gathered to cast lots, asking the spirits for guidance on the plans they had devised to carry out, one of which was attacking the missionaries retreating at Huasang. Three nights in a row, the lot fell on the missionaries, and 120 men were sent to carry out the ruthless murder of the missionaries.

The morning of August 1, 1895, the Vegetarians descended on the unsuspecting missionaries. In a matter of minutes, they killed nine, wounding two children and sending the buildings up in flames. Shielding a baby with her body, the children's nurse died while she was beaten. One of the missionaries, Anna Gordon, was slashed. Two sisters, Eleanor and Elizabeth Saunders, were killed. Their mother, viewing her daughters' martyrdom as an honor, later went to China to take their place. Another woman who was murdered was Lucy Stewart. After the Vegetarians ransacked her room, stealing anything of value, they chased her outside and killed her.

Breaking their code of abstinence from meat, the Vegetarians were said to have feasted on pork and chicken after their slaughter. One source believes there were territorial and political ambitions behind the attack. Another claims the Vegetarians were convinced that one of the missionaries, Robert Stewart, had helped the magistrates find money to pay for soldiers to crush their group.

The murder at Huasang was the first that Protestant missionaries had experienced since their arrival in 1807. But the slaughter did not deter the gospel in China. In a letter dated August 28, 1895, the remaining missionaries with the organization appealed for ten more workers to take the place of those who were killed. Many responded. In addition to the number of missionaries arriving, the martyrdom of these faithful ones created a hunger among the Chinese to experience Christ's salvation.

The only adult missionary to survive the attack, Flora Codrington recovered in England and returned to China. Her deep commitment to the Chinese made a lasting impression, and thousands turned to Christ as a result.

One might say the carnage at Huasang prepared missionaries for what could be the most widespread massacre of foreign missionaries at the hands of a Secret Society, just five years later. Despite the blood that was shed in God's name, He proves to the world that the martyrdom

of His followers only increases compassion and curiosity for the message of salvation that these men and women (and even children) are willing to die for.

A swearing-in ceremony for the Heaven and Earth Society

STORY OF PERSECUTION FROM HISTORY

Wang Zhishen

It was 1900, and Wang Zhishen had just finished his term at Beijing's Methodist University and returned home to be with his family. China's fanatical Secret Society called the Boxers was set loose on society, their fury enflamed with the empress dowager Tzu Hsi's edict. No foreign missionary or Chinese Christian was safe.

Knowing Wang openly professed his Christian faith, his friends urged him to go into hiding.

"No, I cannot," he replied. "I must stay with my family."

As his friends had feared, he was caught and brought before his persecutors, who promised him another chance if he would recant his faith in Christ.

"Wang, please save yourself, and let your friends worship the idols in your place," pleaded one of the village elders. "This will make it easier for you and secure your release!"

"No," replied Wang as he stood before his persecutors. "I will neither burn incense to idols myself nor allow anyone to do it for me. This act would deny my Lord, and I would never dare to look my teachers in the face again."

Unsure of their next move, Wang's persecutors stood there astonished.

"Repent of your sins, and trust in Christ before a worse death overtakes you!" Wang exhorted them.

"Quiet!" ordered one the Boxers.

"Please, repent of your sins, and trust in Christ!" he pleaded.

The sword blade reflected in the light as it cut into Wang's lips, then his tongue, then into every limb.

Even when confronted with death, Wang didn't cease from boldly proclaiming the truth to his persecutors. He joined the tens of thousands of Christians who were martyred at the hands of the Boxers in 1900.

A "Boxer" in 1900

THE BOXER REBELLION

"The foreigners have been aggressive towards us, infringed upon our territorial integrity, trampled our people under their feet...They oppress our people and blaspheme our gods. The common people suffer greatly at their hands, and each one of them is vengeful. Thus it is that the brave followers of the Boxers have been burning churches and killing Christians."

—THE EMPRESS DOWAGER TZU HSI

China had had enough of the foreign invaders. They brought their business, their bad habits, and their beliefs. They were luring Chinese away from their traditions and enticing them to worship a God in heaven. They had to be stopped. One Secret Society did something about it.

Upon China's reluctant signing of the Treaty of Tianjin in 1858, the influence of foreign powers grew, with the British, French, Germans, and Russians all controlling "concessions" along China's ports. At the start of the twentieth century, the country experienced years of bad crops, famine, turmoil, and banditry. Tension was high, and the missionaries and Christians would soon bear the brunt of the blame in what is perhaps China's most ruthless massacre—The Boxer Rebellion.

His country in chaos, Emperor Guangxu tried to bring order through a series of reforms. One source says Emperor Guangxu believed Christian moral and social reforms were the only way to save China from complete foreign domination. He asked Baptist missionary Timothy Richard to help him draw up the reforms. However, on the day Richard arrived, the emperor was overthrown in a coup by a Secret Society called "The Society of Righteous and Harmonious Fists" (what foreign journalists called "The Boxers"), who thought the emperor was selling China out to the foreigners.

The Boxers had a violent hatred of Christians, believing that Christianity offended the spirits of their ancestors. Thinking that the offended spirits would be pacified only by a blood sacrifice, that is exactly what they did with the help of the deposed emperor's aunt, Tzu Hsi. They convinced her that missionaries were stealing Chinese spirits and gouging out the eyes of Chinese children to use in their medicine. The empress dowager took action against the "foreign devils," and on June 21, 1900, issued a secret order to execute all foreigners.

The slaughter began.

Believing that the amulets they wore made them invincible, the Boxers began ravaging towns. In some areas they seized church rosters and went door to door maiming and beheading both missionaries and Chinese Christians, while claiming they could see a cross on the forehead of any true believer. Sometimes they would not allow a Christian's body to be buried for three days, believing that like Jesus, they might also be brought back to life.

One of the most brutal government officials who carried out the empress dowager's orders was Yu Xian, the governor of Shanxi province. (Shanxi became known as "the martyrs' province," from the massive bloodshed that occurred in this province during the Boxer uprising.)

One of the bloodiest slaughters took place in Shanxi's capital, Taiyuan. With the gates of the walled city ordered to be closed, foreigners were trapped.

In late June 1900, mobs set fire to the British Baptist and Sheo Yang Mission compounds. The missionaries and a group of Chinese Christians sought refuge in the Baptist boys' school a half mile away. After they arrived, one of the missionaries, Edith Coombs, realized she left two Chinese schoolgirls behind. Running back to the burning building, she rescued the girls but was caught by the mob and cornered in the flaming structure. Edith's final action was kneeling in the fire as it consumed her.

The missionaries, workers, and children barricaded themselves in the school. On July 9, soldiers arrived and escorted the missionaries to the governor's palace where they joined a dozen Catholic clergy. Any glimmer of hope in being saved was dashed when Yu Xian came running out brandishing his sword shouting, "Kill! Kill!"

The governor ordered the men to be killed first. One man, George Farthing, stepped forward. As he knelt without making a sound, he was killed with one blow of the sword while his wife and three children watched. They were not spared and soon joined him in Christ's presence.

The Boxers killed women and children, as well as nuns and priests who were equally coura-

Boxer Rebellion

geous as they faced the executioner's sword. Finally, the Chinese workers were murdered.

To send a message, Yu Xian had all of their heads placed in cages and displayed on the city wall. Gloating over his mass execution of the missionaries, children, Chinese workers, and Catholic priests and nuns, he boasted to the empress dowager, "Your Majesty's slave caught them as in a net and allowed neither chicken nor dog to escape." The aging empress replied, "You have done splendidly."

Amid the slaughter, government officials sympathetic to the Christians endangered themselves to protect the missionaries and Chinese believers. One governor, Duan Fang, refused to publish the empress dowager's edict to kill Christians. In Jiangsu province, two telegraph officers in Nanjing went so far as to change one Chinese character in the edict from "Kill all the Christians!" to "Protect all the Christians!" They were cut in half for disobeying and changing the edict, yet their bravery saved the lives of hundreds of thousands of Christians in the south, keeping the bloodshed limited to the northern provinces.

At Soping, where missionaries of the Swedish Holiness Union held their annual church conference, Boxers continued to stir up trouble, claiming that the missionaries had swept away rain clouds with a yellow paper broom and were praying to their God for no rain. The missionaries and Chinese Christians with them were chased down, stoned to death, and decapitated. Their heads were hung on the city wall as a warning to all.

Many missionaries who tried to escape were unsuccessful when those sent to protect and escort them gave them up to the Boxers. One such missionary was Carl Lundberg, who tried to flee with fellow missionaries and their children to Mongolia by camel. He wrote, "If we are not able to escape, tell our friends we live and die for the Lord. I do not regret coming to China. The Lord has called me and His grace is sufficient...Excuse my handwriting, my hand is shivering." He and the others were beheaded.

Chinese Christians were not exempt from the slaughter. Most were offered freedom if they would just renounce Christ. Some recanted; many did not. One who refused was a man known as "Faithful" Yen, who with his wife was tied to a pillar in a pagan temple. Soldiers watched as the Boxers brutally beat them with rods and then proceeded to light a fire under them, burning their legs. But the couple still refused to deny Christ. The madmen released Mrs. Yen, but her husband was not so fortunate. The Boxers threw his body onto a pyre and lit it. As his body burned in the flames, one of the soldiers couldn't take the gruesome torture any longer and cursed the Boxers. The soldier was cut to pieces. Enraged at the needless violence, the soldiers then chased the Boxers out of the temple and took Mr. Yen, burned but still barely living, to the magistrate, who threw him in prison where it is believed he died.

Another courageous Chinese believer was Dong Dianfu of Beijing. When word reached him of the approaching Boxers, he sent his wife away to hide. Neighbors revealed their whereabouts, so Dong fled Beijing to seek safety elsewhere. Knowing there was nowhere to hide from the Boxers, he returned to Beijing and went to his father-in-law's house. He was there only minutes before Boxers took him to their headquarters where he was told he could live if he would just renounce Christ. He refused, saying he will believe in Him until death. He knew what was coming next, so he bowed his head and prayed for the Lord to receive his spirit.

When the slaughter finally subsided, more than 30,000 Chinese Christians had been martyred. In *The China Martyrs of 1900*, Robert Coventry Forsyth wrote that "the Boxer massacres produced more Protestant martyrs than all the previous decades of the Protestant Church's history in China. The exact numbers will probably never be known. But we do know that in every corner whither the Boxers came many suffered unspeakable tortures, and many preferred death to apostasy."

Despite the alarming number of deaths, the empress dowager and the Boxers failed to wipe out Christianity. The years following the Boxer

Rebellion created sympathy and compassion toward Christians, opening additional doors for the gospel. One source states that in Jiangxi province, a Protestant missionary reported 20,000 converts in 1901 and 1902. Another says Protestants more than doubled during the six years following the Rebellion. The Catholic Church also grew, almost doubling in size within a decade after the carnage.

What resulted from the massacre was not a spirit of hate and revenge toward the Boxers but one of love and forgiveness. Critics of missions in China who called converts nothing but "rice Christians" (turning to Christ only to have their physical needs met) admitted they were wrong after hearing testimonies of relentless courage in the face of death. A massive number of missionaries also responded to God's call to go and serve in China. Australian missionary David Barratt, who was later martyred, perceived this great turning to Christ after hearing of the massacre in Taiyuan, the capital of Shanxi province, where the most brutal slaughter took place: "Our blood may be as a true center (for the foundation) and God's kingdom will increase over this land. Extermination is but exaltation."

In 1908, the empress dowager Tzu Hsi died, leaving the throne to three-year-old Pu Yi, who would be China's last emperor, ushering in a new era of government under Sun Yat-sen.

WORDS OF COURAGE FROM THE BOXER REBELLION

"I will not. You can do as you please with me, but I will not deny the Lord."

—FIFTEEN-YEAR-OLD CHANG ANG, refusing to recant, immediately before being killed by the sword in Taiyuan

"I don't fear if God wants me to suffer the death of a martyr."

—MINA HEDLUND, in her last letter before being murdered by the Boxers in Soping

"I cannot but believe in Christ: even if you put me to death, I will still believe and follow Him."

—A CHINESE MAN WHO DENIED CHRIST but later told a Boxer magistrate that he repented, and was beaten to death (Rioters cut open his body and extracted his heart, exhibiting it in the magistrate's office.)

*"Well, there is nothing I would
count a greater honor than to wear
a martyr's crown."*

—EDITH SEARRELL's response to a friend while
boarding a ship for China, five years before
being beaten to death by Boxers in Xiaoyi

*"Now you may do as you wish, for I will not
deny Jesus. I am ready."*

—MRS. MENG responding to the Boxers's
demands to deny Jesus by putting on her
best clothes, just before they killed her

*"Pray that God would be sanctified in my
life, and in the lives of all His children
here . . . I long to live a poured-out life unto
Him among these Chinese, and to enter into
the fellowship of sufferings for souls, [as
He] . . . poured out His life unto death for us."*

—MILDRED CLARKE in a letter to her family in 1894
(cut to pieces while she and a fellow missionary
were on a five-day journey to Taiyuan)

END OF THE DYNASTY, RISE OF THE DICTATORS

The Boxer Rebellion had ended, but trouble for Chinese Christians and foreign missionaries had not. Disease hit the mainland, and the country's borders invaded by the Japanese. Added to China's troubles, the Chinese Communist Party (CCP) began making waves along the countryside. And with China's Qing dynasty on the brink of collapse under the leadership of the child emperor Pu Yi, bandits took advantage of the instability and contributed to the chaos.

Eighteen-year-old Andrew Zu of Zheijiang province was martyred at the hands of bandits who tore the young believer to pieces, slicing open his chest in the shape of a cross. A cholera outbreak in 1902 contributed to the slaying of missionaries James Bruce and Henry Lowis in southern Hunan province. Rumors scattered across the city, accusing the two missionaries of poisoning the town's water supply, and of giving the cholera victims poison that they claimed was "medicine." They were beaten to death at Chenzou.

The country's instability finally led to the downfall of the Qing dynasty. With their lucrative trade treaties, foreigners were blamed for supporting the corrupt dynasty and became the targets of the people's hatred that festered after years of resentment. One source says the Manchu dynasty sought refuge with the missionaries, perhaps creating further dissent. At Taiyuan in Shanxi province, the site of vast bloodshed during the Boxer Rebellion, the daughter of the bloodthirsty governor Yu Xian was protected by British Baptists, a beautiful picture of Christ's command to love our enemies.

Yet as the violence escalated and the country filled with turmoil, the church continued to grow.

New Leaders, New Ideas (1920s)

With the downfall of the Qing dynasty in 1911 came the founding of the Republic of China, led by Dr. Sun Yatsen, a Christian who had been educated by missionaries. Britain and the United States refused to rescind their foreign treaties that exploited China's resources. Resentment grew, placing missionaries in danger across the country. In 1923, President Sun Yatsen's followers, called the Nationalists (also known as the Kuo-

mintang), faced a growing revolt in the south. Having been influenced by his Christian education, President Sun instituted reforms to bring back life to the troubled country.

The Russian ambassador pledged to give up his country's treaty rights and help Presi-

Sun Yatsen

dent Sun unify the country while promising not to establish communism in China. While President Sun was befriending the Russians, missionaries from mainline denominations were bringing liberal philosophies and theologies, such as evolution, reducing Chinese confidence in Christianity and preparing the way for Mao's Marxism to make its debut in a matter of years.

With the rising instability that led to chaos and criminal activity, the number of deaths stacked up. One source says that for every missionary who died directly or indirectly from the violence, at least ten Chinese Christians died. One was a former incense maker named Ho. On a trip to sell cloth, he was stopped by thieves who robbed and killed him.

As the communists roamed the countryside, they enlisted the support of peasants in their cause for social equality. With anti-foreign and anti-Christian sentiments still high, Chinese Christians were the targets of the culminating resentment, some of which was elevated by communist agitation. One source says local military and civil authorities often looked the other way when Christians were attacked. In Hunan, Mao's home province, communists seized a believer and charged him with being a "running dog of imperialists" for spreading the teachings of Jesus. The communists told him he was worthy of death. When the believer begged to pray, one of the communists cut off his hand. Knowing he would soon face his Savior, the Christian shouted, "Lord Jesus, receive my spirit!" With those words, he was struck with a sword and died.

President Sun's Nationalists continued their push north in their fight for control of China. In 1925, President Sun Yatsen died, leaving behind a split and conflict-ridden party. The following year the British Navy sailed up the Yangtze Gorges and in a military display of force bombarded the city of Wanxian. Hundreds of Chinese were killed, fanning the flames of anti-foreign hostilities to the point that Chinese Christians severed relations with foreign mission boards.

But 1927 brought what some consider the worst uprising since the Boxer Rebellion. Mission hospitals and schools had to close in China's interior, with missionaries ordered to evacuate to the coast or return home. With the chaos swelling throughout China's provinces, missionaries were more vulnerable to bandits and unscrupulous soldiers as they crossed the deserts and mountainous terrain. Protestant missions lost around 2,500 workers after this mass exodus.

Chiang Kai-Shek

Communists made their contributions to the bloodshed. In the same year, in Haifeng, Guangdong province, communists ruthlessly slaughtered about six hundred Catholics. Many in the town refused to embrace the communists' message and aims, so on November 20, three hundred soldiers and farmers with makeshift weapons brutally attacked the townspeople. Communists inserted iron wires through the noses of village leaders, dragging them through the city streets until they bled to death. Others were thrown into a pond and shot when they surfaced, and a number were doused with gasoline and burned alive.

Chiang Kai-shek succeeded Sun Yatsen as president and sought to purge all communists from his Nationalist army, reversing Sun's policy of friendship with Russia. In 1928, the long civil war between the Nationalists and Mao's communists began.

However, trouble remained for Christians when Chiang was baptized as a Methodist in October 1930, making missionaries and Chinese church leaders an object of communist wrath, as the perception of their association with Chiang's Nationalists deepened. Posters were plastered in cities fueling resentment, claiming that the church housed killers and troublemakers, converts were traitors, and missionaries made slaves of the Chinese.

Many missionaries remained in China, boldly proclaiming the gospel. A missionary in Jiangxi province told communists he was not afraid to die because he knew he was going to heaven. To this, a communist answered, "Let him go to heaven. We will have one less missionary in China to cheat people."

Famines, Plagues, and the Long March (1930s)
Added to the banditry, instability, and communist guerrilla activities were famines and plagues. The situation was so bad, reports surfaced that in one region parents were eating their own children. Those who refused to engage in cannibalism were faced with the choice of either starving or stealing, making it easy for bandits to recruit. These bandits eventually joined ranks with Mao's communists.

The 1930s also witnessed rising Japanese aggression toward China. Baron Tanaka, Japan's Shinto fanatic, and other warlords seized two northern provinces and demanded that five other northern provinces be given independence. Chiang agreed in order to stall his fight with the communists.

In 1934, Mao began the communists' 6,000-mile retreat from southeast China to the northwest in what's been called the Long March, bringing with him and his army of Reds misery and turmoil. Ironically, today's communist propaganda shows the Long March as a time when the masses warmly greeted Mao and his troops as they marched through regions in their one-year retreat from the Nationalists. But the reality is the opposite. Among the thousands the communists killed were members of young churches, many of whom were from minority groups, such as the Qiang. Communists murdered all Qiang pastors and their families and then proceeded to burn their Bibles and destroy their supply of grain. Believers saved some Bibles by stashing them in caves.

In 1937, Japan launched a concentrated attack and by 1939 conquered most of eastern China. With the Japanese occupation, many missionaries were safe, as Japan did not wish to provoke intervention from abroad. However, the Japanese had no qualms with joining the communists in persecuting Chinese Christians. The year 1938 marked another time of horrific violence against Chinese Christians. As communists gained control of large areas of China, thousands of believers were caught up in the fighting between Mao's communists and Chiang's Nationalists. Added to the conflict was the Japanese military trying to seize control. Again, despite the loss of life and property, the church grew.

Facing the Storm (1940s)
The 1940s witnessed greater opportunities for the gospel as communists increased their aggression toward the church.

With Japan's surrender in August 1945, the Nationalists could focus their war efforts on Mao's communists. However, the war with Japan put the communists at an advantage: They had been busy promoting their message among the peasants along the countryside.

In an effort to quash the church, the communists destroyed or confiscated all churches and mission buildings. In 1946, dozens of believers were killed. In Shunde village, Hubei province, communists forcibly disrobed a bishop and twenty priests and nuns and beat them. In 1948, the communists turned the focus of their anti-Christian aggression away from the rural areas to the cities, such as Beijing and Shanghai.

Finally, on October 1, 1949, Mao's communists conquered China, establishing the "People's Republic of China." Mao declared American missionaries "spiritual aggressors." He made it very clear how he would deal with anyone who opposed communism: "This much is certain, whoever wants to oppose the Communist Party must be prepared to be ground to dust. If you are not keen on being ground to dust, you had certainly better drop this opposition. This is our sincere advice to all the anti-Communist 'heroes.'"

Mao Zedong

The communists continued their agenda of wiping out the church in the following decade. With foreign missionaries fleeing the country or being killed, the communists could sharpen their focus on persecuting native Chinese believers, first targeting those associated with Chiang's Nationalists. Many were killed, and others fled to Taiwan.

But the communist crackdown on Chinese Christians only cultivated more courage and a deeper faith. One Christian was tied to a mule and dragged across a field. While he bled, he cried out, "My God, I thank you for having allowed me to be ill-treated as Jesus Christ was, and for His sake!"

Thousands of Christians were arrested and sent to prison where many died; some miraculously survived and were released two decades later. Of those who died, their "official" cause of death was typically disease, accident, or suicide. Christians who bravely remained in China and continued to follow Christ told departing missionaries, "We ask only that you pray for us as we remain to face the storm."

In the late 1950s, Mao closed the doors of China to the world. With missionaries ousted and China's believers hunted down and imprisoned, many anxiously wondered if the church would survive. Years later, the world would be surprised at what they saw and heard.

THE PATRIOTIC CHURCH

"I believe that the real difference between the Three-Self and house church is not . . . legalization, or registration, not even underground and above ground, I believe it is an issue of where their loyalty is: to the government or to their Lord Jesus Christ. For example, the Party would not allow the Three-Self (members) to cross the country to preach the gospel, but the house churches would obey the Great Commission: Take the gospel to the end of the world."

—BOB FU, Chinese dissident and founder of China Aid Association, in a debate on Voice of America (June 3, 2004)

Not long after Mao declared the People's Republic of China, communists focused on controlling institutions that could potentially oppose or compete with their new dictator and ideology. In 1950, a liberal Christian leader named Wu Yao-Tsung and Chinese premier Chou En-lai prepared a "Christian Manifesto," which called on all Chinese Christians to raise their "vigilance against imperialism, to make known the clear political stand of Christians in New China, to hasten the building of a Chinese church whose affairs are managed by the Chinese themselves." About 300,000 Chinese Protestants signed the Manifesto.

Denominations quickly dissolved as the communists formed the Protestant state church—called the Three-Self Patriotic Movement (TSPM)—in the early 1950s.

Ironically, the "three-self" concept originated in 1851 with Henry Venn, founder of the Christian Missionary Society. His concept was intended to guide mission groups as they built indigenous churches on the mission field: self-government, self-reliance, and self-evangelism. But the communists captured it and made it political, originally titling the organization the Three Self Anti-American Aid Korea Patriotic Movement, and demanding the church give her sole loyalty to the government rather than to God.

The TSPM instituted regulations controlling many areas of church life. Today, such rules include which buildings can be used to hold services, which pastors can preach, and which areas of the country can be evangelized. Church activities are restricted to Sundays only; therefore, mid-week meetings and Bible studies are not allowed. TSPM members are not permitted to meet in homes. No one under the age of eighteen can be evangelized or baptized, and members are not allowed any contact with foreign church groups. They are forbidden to read foreign Christian literature or listen to foreign Christian tapes or radio broadcasts.

By 1958, only twelve of the two hundred churches in Shanghai and four of the sixty-five churches in Beijing remained open. However, the government's plan to control Christians and establish a church loyal to the party backfired as believers left the TSPM and started house churches. Unlike missionaries from centuries past, a great number of China's Christians did not seek government approval or "Imperial edicts" for permission to evangelize. Like the apostles, they chose to "obey God rather than men" (Acts 5:29).

Pressure was high for pastors to join the TSPM. One who endured it was Watchman Nee. A slanderous campaign was launched against Nee with accusations that were printed in *Taifeng*, a publication of the Three-Self church. Nee wasn't the only pastor who was targeted. Numerous other house-church pastors were also attacked in the magazine. On April 10, 1952, Nee was arrested and charged as a "lawless capitalist tiger." Offered freedom several times in exchange for his loyalty to the TSPM, Nee refused, and remained in prison until his trial.

On January 30, 1956, 2,500 people gathered at Shanghai for an accusation meeting. Nee's accusers included former leaders of his church who had joined the TSPM. He was found guilty and sentenced to fifteen years imprisonment. Communists had crept into the leadership, and his church later excommunicated him. Told he could secure his freedom if only he would join the TSPM, he again refused. While in prison, his book *The Normal Christian Life* was published and became a best seller. Unfortunately, he would never experience the fruits of his writing, as he died in prison. When his grandniece was notified of his death, she went to his place of incarceration and found a note he had written, saying he had died because of his belief in Christ.

The Protestant church wasn't alone in the government's campaign to control and hamper her growth. Communists attempted to persuade Catholics to start an "independent" Chinese Catholic Patriotic Church but faced opposition. Lashing out at those who refused to comply, the government threw hundreds of priests in prison. Before 1952, about one hundred Chinese clergy perished in prison. In the next two years, four to five hundred more priests were martyred. In 1957, despite resistance, the Catholic Patriotic Association (CPA) was formed. The Pope denounced the CPA, as China demanded loyalty be given to the State, rather than the Pope.

The Bureaucracy

The government needed an arm to enforce state religious policy, so in the 1950s it founded the Religious Affairs Bureau (known today as the State Administration for Religious Affairs, or SARA).

The TSPM became SARA's tool to direct Protestant affairs. SARA identified and manipulated religious workers to fully support Party policy. For example, religious messages must be "compatible with socialism." According to the China

Aid Association, "Pastors are discouraged from preaching about Jesus' divinity, miracles or resurrection, so that believers and non-believers alike can be united together to build a prosperous Socialist China."

When a TSPM or CPA church learns about unregistered (non-TSPM) religious activities, they pass this information along to SARA, which turns these cases over to the Public Security Bureau (PSB). The PSB then carries out raids and arrests participants in these "illegal" activities.

State Seminaries
During Mao's Cultural Revolution (1966–1976), all religious groups were banned, churches were closed, and the TSPM disappeared. Mao died in 1976, and Deng Xiaopeng succeeded him. Alarmed at the growth of underground churches, Deng reopened TSPM churches in 1979 and placed them under the leadership of Bishop Ding Guangxun, a liberal theologian and former Anglican.

Bishop Ding began a theological reconstruction campaign among the government-sanctioned seminaries. More aptly called a "deconstruction" campaign, his agenda included changing the focus of teaching from justification by faith alone in Jesus Christ to justification by love and doing good deeds. Bishop Ding denies the virgin birth and most basic doctrines of Christianity. If any seminary student disagrees with Bishop Ding's theology, he or she is expelled. Knowing the heretical teachings in the state seminaries, house-church Christians have their own "underground" seminaries, or training centers. If caught, they pay dearly.

In April 2007, the PSB raided a house-church training center in Fuyang City, Anhui province. The thirty students were interrogated, and their Bibles were confiscated. Even though they were released, the PSB recorded their names and home addresses, warning them that if they continued to study there rather than at a TSPM seminary, they would be sent to a labor camp.

Today, China operates eighteen seminaries and Bible schools. Nanjing Union Theological Seminary, founded by the TSPM in 1952, is the most prestigious. One believer named Chen attends an underground seminary. Explaining why he risks imprisonment, he stated, "The TSPM slogan is to love country and love Christianity. There is no mention of loving God and other people."

Literature Controls

The government did not stop at placing restrictions on church activities. In the 1980s, the Communist Party started the Amity Press in partnership with foreign-led denominations to control the content and distribution of Christian materials, such as Bibles and commentaries.

Though this sounds like a breakthrough for the church, it's only an illusion. More than half of the resources printed are in English and languages other than Chinese, and many are shipped to other countries for sale. The Bibles and other Christian literature that do remain in China are either given to TSPM members or placed for sale in TSPM outlets, where one source says information on the buyer is collected at the time of purchase. Many buyers are then watched to ensure that their church activities are "legal."

The government's restrictions on churches and Bibles have not hampered the growth of the church. They have only served to deepen the church's commitment to spread the gospel and treasure God's Word in their hearts. One Chinese Christian leader shared:

> No matter which country or where or what type of regime opposes us, God has His supply and way to get the gospel there. This is proven in history many times. China is a growing power, has a strong military and nuclear force and sends men to space, but they cannot stop the Bible. No one can stop God's Word. If the government knew this, they would quit. But they think it is only a book. They think their authority is stronger than God.

Unregistered house-church Christians are ambassadors of Christ, unwilling to yield to the government's demands to use theology that suits

its socialist agenda. Instead, they remain loyal to Jesus—the One who is "ruler over the kings of the earth" (Revelation 1:5).

WORDS OF COURAGE FROM HOUSE-CHURCH CHRISTIANS

"I know the road I have chosen is a difficult one. But after reading the Book of Acts, I have learned about the apostles and their tribulations, the tribulations we all face as Christians. They are a blessing!"

—ZHEN, a Chinese Christian who studies in an unregistered ("illegal") seminary and whose missionary mother has suffered for her faith in Christ

"I had knowledge of Jesus, no relationship with Him."

—BAO, a 23-year-old Christian who grew up in the Three-Self Patriotic Movement (state) church

"I wanted them to hear the truth, to correct some of the false teachings they were receiving in the Three-Self Church."

—EVANGELIST YING, who was arrested and sent to a labor camp for "collaborating with foreigners who intend to subvert the Chinese government" (distributing sermons on CDs to anyone who wanted them, especially Three-Self members)

THE CULTURAL REVOLUTION

Mao was desperate. His Great Leap Forward campaign, to modernize China's economy to compete with the West's, was a failure. Mao's "backyard" steel furnaces that summoned the people to participate in the country's global trading surge forced farmers off the fields, doctors out of the hospital, and teachers out of the classroom, creating widespread famine and fatigue. Meanwhile, the social gap between urban intellectuals and professionals and rural peasants was far too wide. Needing to strengthen his position within the Party, Mao launched the Cultural Revolution (also known as the "Great Revolution to Create a Proletarian Culture") in 1966.

Mao ordered "a comprehensive attack on the 'four old' elements within Chinese society—old customs, old habits, old culture, and old thinking." Student activists, called the "Red Guards," enlisted in the cause for cultural reform and were set loose on society to purge it of anything resembling the "four olds." They arrested government officials, intellectuals, church leaders, and anyone suspected of bourgeois behavior and sent them to communal farms to work alongside peasants. They passed out propaganda leaflets and held debates to criticize those considered "counterrevolutionary." Anything associated with China's pre-communist past was destroyed, including artwork and cultural monuments.

Religion was especially targeted given its ties to Western missionaries. Churches (including the TSPM state churches) were closed, and many of their buildings destroyed. Hundreds of church leaders, including those of the TSPM, were sent to camps for "reeducation through labor." Many died. One young girl imprisoned in 1969 was forced to kneel in the middle of a circle of people, who were ordered to stone her or face death.

"Destroy the old world; establish the new world"

Some Christians refused and were shot at once; others followed orders and killed the girl. It is said that one of those who threw stones at her later turned to Christ.

Another story of great courage during this fanatical bourgeois witch-hunt is told of five Christians, each ordered to dig a hole. When they finished, they were thrown into them, praising God as they were buried alive.

Despite the vast number of martyrs, a remnant of the Church survived.

The Cultural Revolution concluded with Mao's death in 1976 and the arrest of the Gang of Four, which was behind the Cultural Revolution. Led by Mao's wife Jiang Qing, the Gang of Four was positioned to take over leadership of the country after Mao. Deng Xiaoping was later named Mao's successor and brought with him more moderate policies that led China to reopen its doors to the outside world. Christians were also released from prison as a good-faith gesture to Western countries toward human rights and religious freedom. Near the end of the 1970s, state churches were allowed to reopen, the previous years of mass persecution further intensifying the spread of Christ's message of salvation in the hearts of China's people.

HOUSE–CHURCH PATRIOTS

With Mao's successful ousting of missionaries and his henchmen's establishment of state-run churches, some had thought the church was doomed to wither and fade. But they were wrong. Despite threats of imprisonment, many pastors refused to join the communist cause in controlling the church. They were among those who proved the church could not only survive but thrive in the face of threats. Considered patriots, their witness emboldened Christians in China to follow in the steps of the early church and do the unthinkable: obey God rather than men (Acts 5:29). Their names? Pastor Samuel Lamb of Guangzhou and the late Allen Yuan of Beijing.

Their resolve to remain unregistered earned them more than two decades in prison, but their persecution had the opposite effect of the government's intent. As Pastor Lamb has said many times, "Persecution is good for church." Their stories testify to the church's strength and courage when facing imprisonment and harassment for refusing to let the government control what is not theirs, but God's.

Pastor Samuel Lamb
"Under eighteen years of age cannot discern to receive the gospel, therefore they cannot be baptized," said the SARA official to Pastor Lamb.

"Under eighteen years of age also cannot discern to receive Marxism, but they can be Communist Youth League," replied the fragile man of God to the government official.

"Don't criticize other religions," they said.

"Only our God is the true God. All are sinners."

"Are we sinners also?"

"God said, 'All are sinners.' I hope you believe Jesus, too!"

"Next time we talk again."

Pastor Samuel Lamb rarely wasted an opportunity to share the gospel—even with his interrogators. Born October 4, 1924, as Lin Xian Gao, Pastor Lamb's Chinese name bears witness to his life of sacrificial service to the Lord: "Xian" means "to offer to," and "Gao" means "the Lamb of God."

Pastor Samuel Lamb

Having almost died of diphtheria at the age of five and skirted a Japanese bomb at age seventeen, Samuel knew God had a special plan for his life. In 1942, while attending the Alliance Bible Institute in Wuzhou, he memorized the Pauline Epistles. Every morning he committed one paragraph to memory, as well as several psalms. These Scriptures would later come to serve Pastor Lamb during his time in prison.

On April 23, 1950, Pastor Lamb began church meetings every Sunday. Considered a counterrevolutionary, he was arrested September 14, 1955. He and two of his coworkers were jailed for sixteen months and were released in January 1957, when they returned to their work in the church. Then in May 1958, he was arrested again, and this time was held twenty years.

Pastor Lamb served the first five years of his sentence on a farm in Guangdong. Since his body could not endure the hard labor, his leader let him cut the prisoners' hair. Also on the farm was a Baptist preacher who had been allowed to keep a New Testament. Pastor Lamb would borrow the New Testament to copy it, but was caught and sent to Shanxi Taiyuan Coal Mine, where for fifteen years he had the dangerous job of joining coal cars.

Toward the end of his twenty-year sentence, prison officials called on Pastor Lamb to criticize Christianity. One church leader conceded to the government's demands, saying, "I believe no more because Imperialism has cheated me." But Pastor Lamb refused to criticize Christ and boldly told them, "I still believe in the Lord Jesus Christ. If I told you I do not believe, I would be cheating you." The official insisted that Pastor Lamb partake in the criticism. After praying about it, Pastor Lamb returned and instead of criticizing Christ and Christianity, he criticized the liberals who turned their backs on Christ through their false criticism. In response, the leader said, "Oh, you criticized well!"

On May 29, 1978, Pastor Lamb was released from prison, though sadly his wife died two years before his release. In addition to pastoring, he began teaching English. After each lesson, he shared the gospel, and many came to know the Lord. His church began to grow, with about three hundred people coming to each service. The government kept an eye on Pastor Lamb's growing flock and in 1988 called him to their office six times, urging him to join the Three-Self church.

During Lamb's fifth run-in with the government, officials finally said, "Jesus' parents registered. You should do so as well." Pastor Lamb responded to their fuzzy theology saying, "That was the census registration in the Roman Empire; even nonbelievers registered. I have my identification card, election card, and I have a house certificate also. But there is no house-church registration in the Bible."

Today, Pastor Lamb continues to lead his church in Guangzhou and is still watched by the government. He has been visited by foreign dignitaries, journalists, and church leaders from the West as his overcoming testimony has been published throughout the world. But Pastor Lamb has not frowned on or fretted over his sufferings.

He has smiled and joyfully said, "More persecution, more growing."

Allen Yuan

"I could not believe in God, as I couldn't see Him or touch Him. I cannot describe to you exactly how or why. But God revealed Himself into my heart at that moment and gave me the faith to believe in Him. There I turned off the kerosene lights...I knelt on the ground with my hands holding onto my chair. There I confessed my sins and accepted Jesus as my personal Savior. When I turned the light back on, the universe had changed for me."

On December 29, 1932, eighteen-year-old Allen surrendered his life to Christ.

Yuan entered Bible school, and at the end of World War II, he returned to Beijing. The following year he started a church with the help of a Norwegian pastor and saw twenty to fifty people come to Christ and be baptized every year.

Allen Yuan

However, with the founding of the communist Three-Self Patriotic Movement, Brother Yuan was among eleven preachers who refused to join the state-controlled church. In 1958, Yuan, then in his forties, was arrested for "counterrevolutionary crimes" and given a life sentence. He was not alone in his sufferings. His wife endured great hardships as she raised their six children by herself.

Brother Yuan was sent near the Russian border to work on a rice farm. Of his time at the labor camp, he wrote: "It was very cold, food was bad, and the work was hard, but in 22 years I never once got sick. I was thin and wore glasses, but I came back alive; many did not. I also had no Bible for the 22 years, and there were no other Protestant Christians there. I met only four Catholic priests. They were in the same situation I was in; they refused to join the Chinese Catholic Patriotic Association. During those long years in jail, two songs continued to encourage me. One was from Psalm 27, and the other was 'The Old Rugged Cross.'"

In December 1979, Brother Yuan was released from prison, although his run-ins with the police were far from over. On July 8, 2001, three Public Security Bureau officials disrupted a house-church meeting led by Brother Yuan (then eighty-seven years old) and closed it down, sending the attendees home. He was given a serious warning by security officials. Police also went to great lengths to prevent baptisms from taking place. However, in 2003, 397 Christians were baptized in one day in a Beijing river. During another week that same year, 486 were baptized. Brother Yuan and his wife sat along the shoreline joyfully watching the new believers make public statements of their commitment to Christ.

On August 16, 2005, Brother Yuan went to be with the Lord he had so faithfully served. His courageous, unashamed witness for Christ in China is reflected in a plaque hanging above their bed: "Be thou faithful until death, and I will give you the crown of life" (Revelation 2:10).

Allen Yuan and Samuel Lamb are two of many pastors who refused to register with the state-controlled church after its formation in the 1950s. They paid dearly for their bold decision to keep Christ, not the government, as the head of the church, yet the persecution they faced only served to strengthen and expand the church even further.

CHINA'S STRIKE-HARD POLICY

Crime was on the rise. Robberies, rapes, and kid-nappings didn't reflect well on the communist ideal Mao had proposed decades earlier. Too much freedom was causing too much crime, and it had to come to an end.

With Deng Xiaopeng's moderate policies as head of the Communist Party, crime increased dramatically. China responded in 1983 with a new campaign called *Yanda*, meaning "strike hard" or "severe crackdown." This policy implemented the extremes of iron-fisted crackdowns, harsh capital punishment, and speedy execution.

More than one million people were arrested that year, with at least 10,000 executions. Again, Protestants and Catholics were targets of the communists' criminal cleanup campaign. If house-church members refused to register with the government's Three-Self churches or to swear allegiance to the state, they were considered criminals.

For refusing to say, "Chairman Mao is greater than Christ," one Christian doctor was badly beaten. A few days later, police returned to the hospital to see if he had changed his mind but the doctor stood firm: "My Christ is the Lord of lords and King of kings. He has been given a name above all names in heaven, on earth, and under the earth." Officials were enraged. Return-ing days later, they stripped off his clothes and forced him to stand on a bench less than six inches wide. Police mocked the doctor as he quietly meditated on Scriptures. Ten hours later, the doctor remained standing on the narrow bench, quoting verses. Authorities left. A week later he was hanged. Not wasting his last opportunity, the doctor told his persecutors, "My heart is melting for you."

The Communist Party used the media to promote the "strike hard" campaign, communicating the objectives of *Yanda* to dissuade people from committing criminal acts. They also publicized the trials and executions, while praising the atheistic authorities for protecting the people's security.

Since *Yanda*'s emphasis was on swift arrests and sentencing, this anti-crime drive created a high number of forced confessions, false convictions, and wrongful executions. Tibet experienced *Yanda* with crackdowns on activities that promoted independence from China. Christians were again caught up in the anti-crime campaign, as government officials were determined to force unofficial churches to register or face closure. House-church Christians were beaten and harassed, arrested and slapped with fines or imprisonment, while their churches were closed. In Shanghai, over three hundred house churches were shut down in one month alone.

Catholics were not exempt from the roundup. In northern Hubei province, officials pressured churches and clergy to register. The Public Security Bureau arrested clergy and laypeople, while forcing others to stay in their villages, avoid foreigners, stop preaching, and check in with the police one to eight times a day. Churches and prayer houses were destroyed or confiscated.

The 1983 campaign came to a close several months later, only to be reinstated in 1996. The 1996 campaign lasted four months, but this wouldn't be the last time China would experience *Yanda*.

After the U.S. launched its war on terror in response to the attacks of September 11, 2001, China initiated its own version of the war on terror—one that would draw great criticism from the U.S. and other countries. The 2001 campaign was used as a means to restrain political dissent in Tibet and Xinjiang (the area where most of China's Muslims reside) and surpassed the length of the previous two.

Despite the government's attempts to control the church through anti-crime crusades, a revolution would rouse the nation to a stand-off in Tiananmen Square.

CHINA TODAY

A Dangerous Woman

Her work was dangerous. With the government permitting only one Christian magazine to be published, Li Ying knew that wasn't sufficient to encourage believers across China. Something needed to be done, and she did it. In the course of four years, her publication became a threat to the government, and they would do whatever it took to stop her—even sentence her to death.

As a youth, Li knew the physical perils of following Christ. In 1983, Christians were caught up in nationwide crackdowns on crimes, and Li's father was arrested. Despite her father's imprisonment, Li desired to preach. She attended training seminars and taught theological courses. Some members of the government-run Three-Self churches requested her teaching—something that was risky both to her and to those she taught, as many withdrew from the Three-Self church.

Li had her first run-in with police when she traveled to Sichuan province for a retreat. Tipped off by a villager, Public Security Bureau (PSB) officers surrounded the meeting house. Each person was fined. Police forced Li to kneel on a bench the entire night. She and the others were later released after police failed to find criminal evidence.

Three years later, Li assisted a coworker who was fleeing the police. Carrying her friend on her bike, Li sped away only to be captured. She endured forced labor for one year, pasting paper boxes. After her release, she continued leading fellow believers in studying the Scriptures.

In 1997, Li started a Christian newsletter. The circulation of the newsletter increased, but her writing did not go unnoticed by the Chinese government. Four years into her work on the publication, Li was arrested as she arrived at a meeting. During five days of interrogation, police beat her with an electric baton, forced her underwater, and tortured her in other ways. Thrown in a cell with three other women, Li used the opportunity to share the gospel and to encourage believers in nearby cells.

After eight months the day of her trial finally arrived, and three days later she received the shocking sentence: the death penalty. Very heavy-hearted, Li cried out to God.

Almost one year later, she was retried on orders of the Hubei Provincial Supreme Court. Her sentence was reduced to fifteen years in prison. Li was transferred to Wuhan Women's Prison, where she is forced to work fifteen hours a day on materials for export.

Once the world learned of Li's imprisonment, letters of encouragement poured in to her, as well as protests to the government. On one visit to the prison, Li's mother was asked by the warden, "How many relatives do you have in America?"

Though grateful that her death penalty was revoked, she experienced another setback when her family went to the prison only to be met with demands to pay a fee. The warden told them, "You are not permitted to have a lunch party …We cannot hear what you talk if you have a party together." Li could talk to them only by phone.

As her mother explained, Li knows that "to follow the Lord means suffering. Her suffering for Jesus is a glory." Li knew her work on the publication was dangerous, but refusing to print words of encouragement to strengthen Christians in China carried far greater risk.

Li Ying

TIANANMEN SQUARE: DEMONSTRATIONS GONE WRONG

"This [demonstration] is a planned conspiracy and a disturbance. Its essence is to, once and for all, negate the leadership of the CPC [the Communist Party] and the socialist system. This is a serious political struggle confronting the whole party and the people of all nationalities throughout the country."

—"It is Necessary to Take a Clear-Cut Stand Against Disturbances" editorial in *Renmin ribao (People's Daily),* April 26, 1989

He gave them hope, and now it was gone. Accused of being too lenient on student uprisings around the country, Hu Yaobang, the General Secretary of the Communist Party, was forced to resign. Gone were their dreams for government reforms and freedom. When he died two years later, all hell seemed to break loose.

On April 15, 1989, students gathered in Tiananmen Square to commemorate Hu, and used the opportunity to make demands for freedom. Days passed, and the students continued to demonstrate. One source says a hundred thousand had gathered, with several hundred leading a hunger strike.

On May 19, students learned of the government's plan to institute martial law. That evening, Premier Li Peng delivered a speech calling for an end to the turmoil. In typical communist fashion, he accused the demonstrators of spreading "many rumors, attacking, slandering, and abusing principal leaders of the party and state."

Finally, the government took military action to remove students from the square. On June 3 and 4, tanks and armored personnel carriers rolled toward the square while troops, armed with automatic weapons, shot any civilians who attempted to impede them from moving forward. Police fired tear gas on the crowds. Civilians retaliated by setting fire to armored personnel carriers, and by throwing rocks, bottles, and Molotov cocktails at soldiers.

The image of the man standing before the tanks will forever be etched in the minds of those witnessing this revolution, eerily symbolizing the lone voice for democracy in the face of a dictatorship bent on controlling the masses.

Mass Arrests and Imprisonment
Days after what many called "Bloody Sunday" and the "Beijing Bloodbath," the sound of bullets faded. Thousands were rounded up, questioned, and jailed by police, while many students fled the country. Others went into hiding.

Dissidents were missing. Police were sent to universities, tearing down anti-government posters and detaining students. In declaring martial law, Beijing issued two directives making independent student and worker groups illegal and labeling their leaders counterrevolutionaries, while the media encouraged citizens to report on rioters. Sources conflict on the number of dead and wounded, with estimates ranging from the hundreds to the thousands.

Many house-church leaders were targeted in the roundup and imprisoned. Since unauthorized gatherings were banned, house-church Christians experienced increased difficulties in meeting, but they still found ways to share the gospel and fellowship. Others were targeted for arrest, like evangelist Ten Su. As soon as he stepped off a train—caught with a bag of Bibles and relief money—he was arrested and jailed for several months. After his release, he risked arrest and imprisonment while he courageously continued his Christian work.

Tiananmen Square

Tiananmen's Aftereffects

The United States responded to Tiananmen Square when President George H. W. Bush announced minor diplomatic sanctions on China, and the U.S. Congress opposed China's renewal of Most Favored Nation (MFN) status. (The President must inform Congress annually of his desire to renew or deny the MFN status of communist countries.) Adding to China's trade woes, approval of its application to the World Trade Organization was slowed after the crackdown.

Upon Clinton's election to office, he renewed China's MFN status, claiming it would open up China to democratic and political reforms through the economy.

Has China changed its ways as it has been forced to do business with the world? Or has it remained "business as usual," adding more Christians to its blood-stained trail? The answer would arise years later as a crackdown on cults led to the arrest and imprisonment of house-church Christians across the nation.

EVIL CULTS: AN OLD TACTIC WITH A NEW NAME

As the twentieth century was coming to a close, unregistered house churches were still on the rise. China released secret documents about suppressing religious groups that refuse to submit to state-controlled bodies. The government admitted losing the battle to control religious expression, so it adjusted its line of attack: label these groups as "evil cults" in order to shut them down. Unregistered house-church Christians were targeted in "cult" clean-ups. This was nothing new. Centuries earlier, Christians were included in crackdowns on Secret Societies. The government system and leaders have changed, their methods haven't.

Posters were hung and students were warned, as everyone from kindergarten on up was required to study the dangers of cults. One book says, "When evil cults cheat people, pretend to care about you, and make you feel very close to them, you are trapped without being aware." The book shows a man called "Mr. Wei," who "participates in evil cult activities, cheats others, and runs to outside townships to distribute evil cult pamphlets." The adjoining picture shares the consequences for participating in and propagating cult activities: "After the evil cult was eradicated, Wei was put on trial. He was very remorseful. He explained in the court, 'I am guilty and should be punished because of my crime.'"

China's anti-cult campaign required every citizen to inform the government of any cult activities, with rewards of up to U.S. $500. Reminiscent of China's strike-hard policy against crime,

三、邪教骗人

1、假装关心人

邪教骗人时，假装关心你，让你觉得很亲近，不知不觉上了当。

①农民魏某，因病做了手术，生活更加困难。一天，魏家来了两个神秘的人，对魏"安慰"一番，魏某很感激。

②这两人逐渐成了魏某的"知心朋友"。魏某受骗入了邪教，交了300元钱和600公斤小麦。

③魏某积极参加邪教活动，又欺骗他人，还跑到外地散发邪教传单。

④邪教被取缔后，魏某被绳之以法。他十分后悔。

Chinese government posters warning of evil cults

Christians like seventy-four-year-old Chen Jiang-mao continue to be swept up in the crackdown.

Chen was arrested and sentenced to four years at Sanxia Prison in Chongqing City. Part of his crime was sending his granddaughter to Bible training school, which was illegal because she was younger than eighteen. Charged with "using an evil cult to obstruct the law" and undermining the educational system with "illegal evangelistic activities," Brother Chen then led fifty inmates to Christ. For this, more than ten prison guards beat him while yelling, "You make the Communist Party lose face! We'll beat you to death, you old man!" His body was so broken he was unable to walk or use the restroom and was hospitalized. But his spirit was not broken. He was later released from prison.

The government continued to issue documents against "evil cults."

In 2005, China Aid Association received secret documents from the city of Datong in Shanxi province and the city of Shayang in Hubei province, outlining China's systematic agenda of discrimination against religious "cults." Prepared by The Offices of the Leadership Group to Prevent and Handle Cultic Activities of the Chinese Communist Party, the documents ambiguously define "cults," allowing their enforcement to violate the scant religious freedom believers in China have.

House-church leader Gu Changrong, age fifty-four, of Fushun city in Liaoning province was arrested on March 14, 2007, for "evil cult activities" after she shared her faith with the secretary of the Communist Party in her village. She was accused of "poisoning Communist Party members with the Christian message" and sentenced to one year of reeducation through labor for "using evil cult organizations to obstruct the exercising of state laws." Gu is serving her sentence at Ma San Jian Labor Camp.

As China's communists found new ways to try to crush the church, the number of people who turned to Christ grew. Their resolve and spirit remain like that of Brother Chen Jiangmao, who shared with his daughter after he was beaten by police, "It is an honor to suffer for Christ. Pray for me. Take heart because the Lord is with me. My chains will increase the Kingdom."

CHINA'S NEW FACE AND OLD WAYS

"Some of the perceptions in the western world that things in China are loosening up within [the core power center]; that is wrong..., the inside is tighter now, even tighter than five years ago."

—DR. PERRY LINK, professor of East-Asian Studies at Princeton University

With Beijing hosting the 2008 Olympics and China positioned as an economic superpower, the country's development is turning heads. Ted C. Fishman writes in *China, Inc.*: "China has...become the world's largest maker of consumer electronics, pumping out more TVs, DVD players, and cell phones than any other country...No country has ever before made a better run at climbing every step of economic development all at once."

Despite America's hope of political reform through economic freedoms, China has learned to play the global trading game while keeping its human rights violations hidden...as much as possible. With the upcoming Olympics, the situation has not improved. Zhou Yongkang, Minister of Public Security, announced the need to "strike hard" at hostile forces within the country's borders and abroad in order to create an amicable society to host the 17th Communist Party Congress and the Beijing Olympics.

Much like in the previous strike-hard policies, China's house-church Christians are often caught up in the crackdown on terrorists, cult groups, and community "cleanups." After Beijing was announced as host of the 2008 Olympics, the government demolished the family home of seventy-seven-year-old house-church Christian Mrs. Shuang Shuying. Because the home was close to Tiananmen Square, communists viewed it as "a politically defiant dwelling" and claimed it would hurt the "new Beijing, new Olympics." The family was moved to a suburb and detained in a facility where the family was supervised around the clock and was beaten.

When Shuang and her son went to the Beijing People's Representatives Conference to protest their home being destroyed, they were beaten and her son was sentenced to six months in prison.

Shuang and her husband then returned to appeal their rights and their son's release. She was arrested and later convicted of "willfully damaging public and private property" for damaging government property—including the hood of a police car when it tried to run her over and she used her cane to protect herself. While in prison, she has faced brutal treatment.

More Shifting Strategies

China Aid Association (CAA) notes the great challenge to obtain the exact number of persecution cases in China due to the country's geographical size, population, and government efforts at concealment. Such information would add to its already troubled human rights record. The Chinese government blocks and monitors the Internet, making it a challenge for citizens to share information with the outside world. Some are reluctant to report persecution, fearing a backlash from the government, and many aren't aware that groups exist in the free world to raise awareness of Christian persecution.

Based on known cases, CAA reports that raids on house churches decreased in 2006, as the government shifted strategies. PSB officials have raided house churches and detained leaders for extended periods, while most church members were interrogated on site and released. House-church leaders have been charged with criminal activities, while house churches are still classified as "evil cults." Henan house-church leader Zhang Rongliang was given a seven-and-a-half-year prison sentence for "illegally crossing the national border and fraudulently obtaining a passport" in June 2006. CAA's 2007 report indicated an increased number of house churches facing government persecution, but a decreased number of people sentenced to imprisonment.

China may have a new face, but it continues its old ways of striking hard on the church while attempting to present a good image to the world through its exports and the red carpet it will roll out for the Beijing Olympics. However, Christians in China are boldly sharing the gospel despite the government's efforts to deceive the world and control the church through criminal accusations and new tactics.

CHINA TODAY

A Crime of "Economics"

His case was to be dealt with severely and harshly. "Yan Ban!" were the words one official in Beijing wrote on his directive. Cai Zhuohua's case had been called the most serious one "on overseas religious infiltration since the founding of the People's Republic of China." All this for a man who was printing Bibles and Christian literature without a license.

It was 2004, and Pastor Cai Zhuohua had just finished his weekly leadership meeting at a church. As he waited for his bus, three plainclothes policemen grabbed him and shoved him into a van. His cell phone was confiscated. In the weeks that followed, authorities would use it to uncover an underground seminary and shut it down. Word reached Cai's wife and her brother-in-law that there was trouble. They went into hiding, and Cai's four-year-old son went into the care of his grandmother.

Police were convinced Pastor Cai hadn't acted alone. They raided a company registered to Cai's wife and were shocked at their discovery: more than 200,000 printed pieces of Bibles and other Christian literature. The police confiscated computers and arrested six employees in addition to another person associated with Cai's work. The workers were questioned and released the following day, but Cai's wife and her brother-in-law weren't so fortunate. They were discovered and arrested.

Furious that this pastor had printed so much forbidden literature under their noses, government officials decided to take a different approach on this case: charge Cai and his conspirators with tax evasion or illegal business management rather than with illegal religious activity. These charges would mean a possible life sentence while allow-

Pastor Cai Zhouhua

ing the government to deny religious motivation for the prosecution. Authorities thought they could pull it off. They claimed Cai illegally printed these materials and sold them without paying appropriate taxes. They were almost successful. During interrogation, police tortured Cai and threatened his wife and her brother-in-law with torture, enabling them to secure false testimonies that the three profited from "illegal business practices." When they were finally put on trial, all three revoked their confessions, saying they were forced to sign under duress.

Cai's lawyer argued that the printed materials "promote social stability, since they teach people about kindness, mercy, and love," but the judge would not permit any arguments about religious issues. "This has nothing to do with religion," Judge You Tao said from the bench. "This is an economic crime." The defense fought back but was allowed only one witness to testify: an elderly Christian woman who said she received literature from Pastor Cai without being asked for payment.

Judge Tao handed down the sentence: Pastor Cai was to spend three years in prison, his wife two years, and her brother-in-law a year-and-a-half. They were fined a total of 370,000 Yuan (almost U.S. $50,000) for printing more than 200,000 copies of Christian literature. The State Administration of Religious Affairs (SARA) director, Ye Xiaowen, went so far as to publicly accuse Pastor Cai of printing forty million copies and selling three million—a blatant lie!

Cai was transferred several times and each time endured forced labor making exportable products like footballs and handbags. None of his relatives were allowed to visit him, and he was not allowed to have a Bible.

He was released in September 2007 after serving his sentence, but his troubles are far from over. He is required to report to the Public Security Bureau (PSB) office once a month and has been warned not to speak out or attend church services.

Some will claim that Pastor Cai could have avoided prison if only he would have obeyed the government and requested a license to print the literature. But Pastor Cai knew better: Only the government's Amity Press is allowed to print religious materials. His request would have been denied. The need for Christian materials to equip believers is great, and he was willing to face the consequences. His mother said it well: "The [Communist] Party wants us to obey only them. They don't want people to hear the real words of love, of God...We are simple people, but we do know this: In the Bible, it says follow your leaders, but first follow your God."

China will continue to look for new ways to stop the church while keeping its human rights record "clean." Meanwhile, Pastor Cai is happy to be together with his family again.

CONCLUSION:
THE TRAIL CONTINUES

Since Christianity's first recorded arrival, the church has experienced both times of favor and times of opposition and persecution at the hands of empresses, emperors, Secret Societies, fanatical groups, and communist dictators. There were periods during Christianity's history in China that the church seemed extinct, but a remnant remained, following the truths taught by those who dared to bring the gospel to a land traditionally apprehensive to anything foreign.

With the fall of communism in Eastern Europe during the late 1980s and early 1990s, many wondered if China would follow suit. The trade and economic concessions granted to China bore political hopes of improving China's human rights record, but they have merely created a world superpower that continues to deny its people complete freedom and justice.

Despite China's lack of liberties, the church is growing and sharing about the eternal freedom and justice only found through a relationship with Jesus Christ. Unwilling to wait for permission from their atheistic, communist government, house-church Christians are leading people to Christ in record numbers. They are willing to accept the punishment for their "crimes," be it prison, hard labor, or even death—like Jiang Zongxiu, who was beaten to death for distributing gospel tracts in the village market, and Li Ying, who is in prison for printing a Christian magazine without government permission.

Some Western voices say that China's Christians do have freedom to worship. These groups claim the government's Amity Press and state-run churches are the government's way of extending their hand of good will to allow Christians a place to worship. But are China's Christians truly free to worship? It is true that some progress has been made toward religious freedom, although China has a long way to go. The number of Bibles that Amity Press prints in a given year is still far from sufficient. Amity Press celebrated printing its 50 millionth Bible in 2007. The number sounds quite impressive, though disappointing when one realizes that this number was produced in *two decades.*

With China's population at 1.3 billion and Christians estimated at 7.25 percent of the population, meaning approximately 94 million believers, the number of Bibles printed (with about one-fifth shipped overseas) is nowhere close to getting into the hands of every Christian.

Zhou Heng was arrested for conducting an "illegal business operation," when he went to pick up 3 tons of imported Bibles in Xinjiang. Is that religious freedom? And is it religious freedom when Chinese attend state-run churches, trust in Christ, are baptized, and then questioned by their employers about their pursuit of a "primitive" belief? Stay informed of today's persecuted church in China, and you decide.

Take Part in Their Journey

The stories of persecution will continue as believers in China take Christ's Great Commission seriously and refuse to add their names to the communists' registry for monitoring purposes. The government's attempts to quash the church will continue to change as it struggles to find new ways to stop what simply cannot be stopped. What can we do as we hear of such injustices and atrocities against Christ's Body? As the late Pastor Allen Yuan shared with VOM-Australia workers prior to his death, "Pray first for the lost millions of China. Secondly, pray for the newcomers and new believers. Third, please pray for the leaders of our country."

As our brothers and sisters in Christ secretly minister and sit behind bars for their witness, you can pray for their encouragement and strength. Ask God to raise up leaders grounded in the Word to pastor the new and growing congregations springing up across the country. Pray for creative ways to get Bibles and other Christian materials to believers in China. Pray for foreign workers who travel to China to help meet the vast spiritual needs of the believers. And pray that government leaders in China will experience Christ's love through members of His Body and will hunger for and seek the Truth.

There are many other ways you can help believers in China. Go to www.prisoneralert.com to sign up to receive e-mails about Christians who are imprisoned for their faith in Christ. There is a place on the site to send e-mails to these believers in prison as well as a place to send a note to government officials of their country to protest their imprisonment.

You can also mail Scriptures to people in China through VOM's Bibles Unbound program. For a small, monthly cost, you will receive Scriptures in the native language, along with envelopes, postage, and addresses for mailing.

Finally, subscribe to The Voice of the Martyrs' free, monthly newsletter, which contains updates on today's persecuted church and ways you can tangibly help them, pray for them, and tell their stories to your friends and family.

Now that you know the history, struggles, and victories of many who have journeyed on China's blood-stained trail, will you join in the "fellowship of sufferings" of our persecuted family (Philippians 3:10)? It's a relationship that will last into eternity as we serve with them on the blood-stained trail.

FOR FURTHER READING

The following sources are a selection of those consulted in the writing of this book and are recommended for further reading and research.

De Sègur, Monseigneur. *Familiar Instructions and Evening Lectures on All the Truths of Religion, Volume II* (London: Burnes & Oates, 1881).

Forsyth, Robert Coventry (Ed.). *The China Martyrs of 1900* (London: The Religious Tract Society, 1904).

Hattaway, Paul. *China's Christian Martyrs* (Grand Rapids, MI: Monarch Books, 2007).

Hefley, James and Marti. *By Their Blood* (Grand Rapids, MI: Baker Books, 1996).

Huc, M. L'Abbé. *Christianity in China, Tartary, and Thibet, Volume I* (London: Longman, Brown, Green, Longmans, & Roberts, 1857).

Moffett, Samuel Hugh. *A History of Christianity in Asia, Volume I: Beginnings to 1500* (Maryknoll, NY: Orbis Books, 1998).

Moffett, Samuel Hugh. *A History of Christianity in Asia, Volume II: 1500 to 1900* (Maryknoll, NY: Orbis Books, 2005).

Spence, Jonathan D. *The Search for Modern China* (New York: W. W. Norton & Company, Inc., 1990).

The Voice of the Martyrs monthly publication.

Walsh, W. Pakenham. *Modern Heroes of the Mission Field* (London: Hodder and Stoughton, 1882).

Online Resources
China Aid Association Web site: www.chinaaid.org.

"China: Human Rights Developments." Human Rights Watch Publications. <www.hrw.org/reports/1997/WR97/ASIA-03.htm>. Accessed June 22, 2007.

"The Olympics Countdown—repression of activists overshadows death penalty and media reforms." Amnesty International USA. <www.amnestyusa.org/document.php?lang=e&id=ENGASA170152007>. Accessed June 28, 2007.

Richelson, Jeffrey T. and Michael L. Evans (Prepared by). "Tiananmen Square, 1989: The Declassified History." National Security Archive Briefing Book No. 16. June 1, 1999. <www.gwu.edu/~nsarchiv/NSAEBB/NSAEBB16/index.html>. Accessed July 2, 2007.

The Voice of the Martyrs' Web site: www.persecution.com.

RESOURCES

The Voice of the Martyrs has many books, videos, brochures, and other products to help you learn more about the persecuted church. In the U.S., to order materials or receive our free monthly newsletter, call (800) 747-0085 or write to:

The Voice of the Martyrs
P.O. Box 443
Bartlesville, OK 74005-0443
www.persecution.com
thevoice@vom-usa.org

If you are in Australia, Canada, New Zealand, South Africa, or the United Kingdom, contact:

Australia:

Voice of the Martyrs
P.O. Box 250
Lawson NSW 2783
Australia

Website: www.persecution.com.au
Email: thevoice@persecution.com.au

Canada:

Voice of the Martyrs, Inc.
P.O. Box 608
Streetsville, ON L5M 2C1
Canada

Website: www.persecution.net
Email: thevoice@vomcanada.org

New Zealand:
>Voice of the Martyrs
>P.O. Box 5482
>Papanui, Christchurch 8542
>New Zealand
>
>Website: www.persecution.co.nz
>Email: thevoice@persecution.co.nz

South Africa:
>Christian Mission International
>P.O. Box 7157
>1417 Primrose Hill
>South Africa
>
>Email: cmi@icon.co.za

United Kingdom:
>Release International
>P.O. Box 54
>Orpington BR5 9RT
>United Kingdom
>
>Website: www.releaseinternational.org
>Email: info@releaseinternational.org